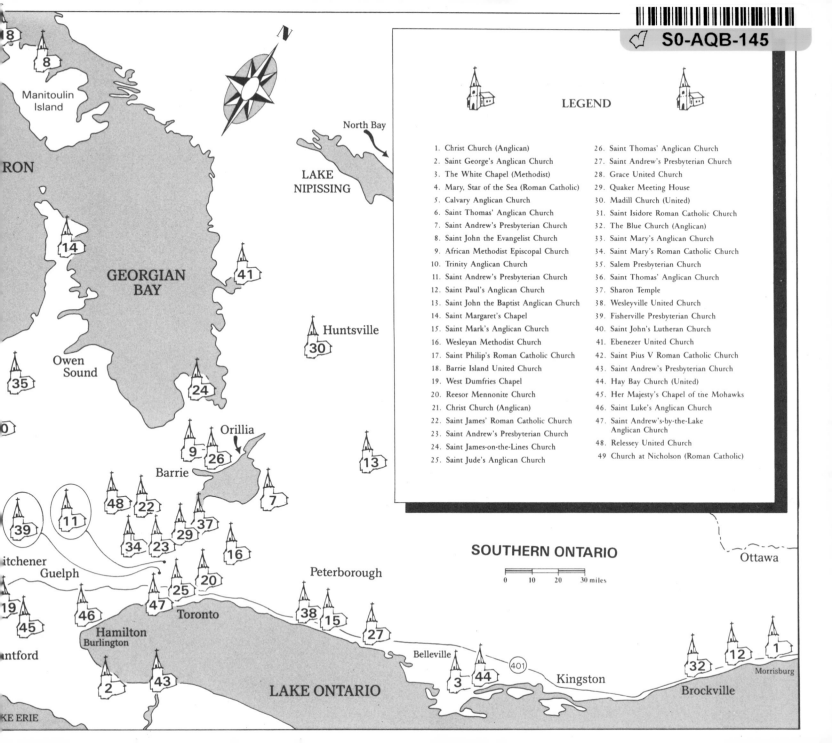

N

LEGEND

1. Christ Church (Anglican)
2. Saint George's Anglican Church
3. The White Chapel (Methodist)
4. Mary, Star of the Sea (Roman Catholic)
5. Calvary Anglican Church
6. Saint Thomas' Anglican Church
7. Saint Andrew's Presbyterian Church
8. Saint John the Evangelist Church
9. African Methodist Episcopal Church
10. Trinity Anglican Church
11. Saint Andrew's Presbyterian Church
12. Saint Paul's Anglican Church
13. Saint John the Baptist Anglican Church
14. Saint Margaret's Chapel
15. Saint Mark's Anglican Church
16. Wesleyan Methodist Church
17. Saint Philip's Roman Catholic Church
18. Barrie Island United Church
19. West Dumfries Chapel
20. Reesor Mennonite Church
21. Christ Church (Anglican)
22. Saint James' Roman Catholic Church
23. Saint Andrew's Presbyterian Church
24. Saint James-on-the-Lines Church
25. Saint Jude's Anglican Church

26. Saint Thomas' Anglican Church
27. Saint Andrew's Presbyterian Church
28. Grace United Church
29. Quaker Meeting House
30. Madill Church (United)
31. Saint Isidore Roman Catholic Church
32. The Blue Church (Anglican)
33. Saint Mary's Anglican Church
34. Saint Mary's Roman Catholic Church
35. Salem Presbyterian Church
36. Saint Thomas' Anglican Church
37. Sharon Temple
38. Wesleyville United Church
39. Fisherville Presbyterian Church
40. Saint John's Lutheran Church
41. Ebenezer United Church
42. Saint Pius V Roman Catholic Church
43. Saint Andrew's Presbyterian Church
44. Hay Bay Church (United)
45. Her Majesty's Chapel of the Mohawks
46. Saint Luke's Anglican Church
47. Saint Andrew's-by-the-Lake Anglican Church
48. Relessey United Church
49. Church at Nicholson (Roman Catholic)

Manitoulin Island

LAKE NIPISSING

North Bay

GEORGIAN BAY

Owen Sound

Huntsville

Orillia

Barrie

SOUTHERN ONTARIO

0   10   20   30 miles

Peterborough

itchener

Guelph

Toronto

Hamilton
Burlington

ntford

Belleville

(401)

Kingston

Morrisburg

Brockville

LAKE ONTARIO

Ottawa

KE ERIE

# STEEPLE CHASE
## ONTARIO'S HISTORIC CHURCHES

# STEEPLE CHASE
## ONTARIO'S HISTORIC CHURCHES

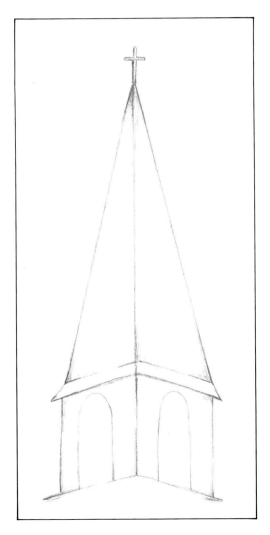

James and Susan Preyde

## THE BOSTON MILLS PRESS

**Canadian Cataloguing in Publication Data**

Preyde, Jim
  steeple chase: Ontario's historic churches

Includes bibliographical references.
ISBN 1-55046-030-7

1. Churches – Ontario – History. 2. Churches –
Ontario – Pictorial works. I. Preyde, Susan. II, Title.

NA5246.05P74 1990      726.509713      C90-094486-2

Published by:
THE BOSTON MILLS PRESS
132 Main Street
Erin, Ontario N0B 1T0
(519) 833-2407
FAX (519) 833-2195

Edited by Noel Hudson
Designed by John Denison & Lexigraf
Cover designed by Gillian Stead
Typography by Lexigraf, Tottenham
Printed in Singapore

American Association
for State and Local History
Award of Merit

Winners of the
Heritage Canada
Communications Award

The publisher wishes to acknowledge the financial assistance
of The Canada Council, the Ontario Arts Council and the Office
of the Secretary of State.

# Contents

*St. George's Anglican Church, Ball's Falls.*

# Introduction

This collection of photographs is the result of our efforts over many years and many miles. It began as an interest in our history and in the beauty of churches in their unique settings. Support and encouragement from our family and friends led to a decision to have the collection published.

Churches were chosen as much for their appearance as for their historical value. Some churches of historical worth are not included simply because they were inadvertently by-passed in our travels, or perhaps did not appeal to our subjective aesthetic values of the moment. The weather, the play of the light on the building, the overall mood – many factors were taken into consideration in the final choice of the churches included here.

Each of these photographs hold special memories for us. Our hope is that you, the reader, can extract from them some of the peace and serenity that existed when they were taken.

## Christ Church (Anglican)
### *Stormont, Dundas and Glengarry County*

This church was moved from Moulinette in the 1950s to prevent its loss by flooding during the Saint Lawrence Seaway project, which put the town under water. Christ Church (Anglican), which saw its first service in 1837, is now on display at the Upper Canada Village near Morrisburg.

## Saint George's Anglican Church
### Niagara Region

Saint George's Anglican Church was built in 1864 in Hannon, south of Hamilton. There, services were held for a century before the church was moved to its present location at Ball's Falls Historical Park and Conservation Area. Saint George's is now on display with other 19th-century buildings.

## The White Chapel
*Prince Edward County*

The White Chapel, just north of Picton, is a Methodist meeting house built in 1809. Annual services give this meeting house the distinction of being used as a place of worship longer than any other Methodist church in the province.

## Mary, Star of the Sea
*Essex County*

Pelee Island is Canada's most southerly township and home to this Roman Catholic church. Named Mary, Star of the Sea, the church celebrated its centennial in 1987. Surrounded by tall, majestic trees, the Star of the Sea now holds only summer services.

## Calvary Anglican Church
*Essex County*

The north end of Pelee Island is the site of the Calvary Anglican Church. Dedicated Methodist in 1898, it became a United church in 1925, and in 1942 was taken over by the Anglican Diocese. The Methodist church from the south end of the island was attached to this building in 1946 and became the parish hall. This solid church is constructed of local stone with attractive leaded stained-glass windows. The window over the main entrance identifies the structure as "The Christians' Home."

## Saint Thomas'
### *Cochrane District*

By Ontario's standards, the town of Moose Factory is quite ancient, established in 1673 as a Hudson's Bay Company fort and trading post. Its Anglican church, Saint Thomas', is comparatively new, constructed in 1864. The native Cree influence is evident in many forms. Native life is vividly depicted in the colourful stained-glass windows and the altar cloth is of moosehide with detailed beadwork. For the first several decades of its existence the church was plagued with spring floods and break-ups. More than once the church had to deal with a deluge of mud. Holes were drilled in the floor to allow drainage and prevent the structure from floating away, as it had on one occasion.

TO THE GLORY OF GOD AND IN THANKFUL RECOGNITION OF JOHN HORDEN, 1851–1893, AS MISSIONARY, TRANSLATOR AND TEACHER; DEACON, PRIEST, AND BISHOP IN THE CHURCH OF GOD PLACED BY THE MEMBERS OF THE W.A. OF THE DIOCESE OF MOOSONEE, 1961.

## Saint Andrew
*Durham Region*

    The northern Durham Region township of Thora is home to one of the numerous Presbyterian churches named for Saint Andrew. This neo-Classical structure of limestone and granite was completed in 1853. Its sturdy and enduring appearance notwithstanding, it was replaced less than 30 years later by a new Saint Andrew's in nearby Beaverton. The church now provides only summer services.

## Saint John the Evangelist Church (Anglican)
### *Manitoulin District*

Saint John the Evangelist Church in Kagawong actually started life as a warehouse in 1898. It did not see religious activities until December 1936, when it was sold to the Anglican Diocese of Algoma for one dollar. Perched on a rocky shore overlooking Manitoulin Islands' North Channel, the church has a distinctive maritime flavour. Inside, a ship's life preserver adorns the wall. The church's pulpit is the restored bow of a boat that was wrecked in the North Channel in the summer of 1965, tragically taking the lives of its passengers.

## African Methodist Episcopal Church
### Simcoe County

This simple frame-and-log building is the African Methodist Episcopal Church, constructed in 1849 in Oro Township. The years between 1830 and 1850 witnessed the migration of several black families from the United States. They formed a community in this area and brought with them their customs and faiths. As neighbouring white settlements grew and prospered, the black congregation was absorbed into their fold. Their small church, which also served as a school, still stands as a humble monument to their beginnings in a new land. Today the grounds are well kept and the building's whitewashed interior contains but a few benches and a simple lectern.

## Trinity Anglican Church
*Elgin County*

The Trinity Anglican Church at Port Burwell was completed in 1837. The financial benefactor of the project was Colonel Mahlon Burwell, the founder of the town. The frame structure is a good example of early Gothic Revival architecture.

## Saint Andrew's Presbyterian Church
*York Region*

Saint Andrew's Presbyterian Church in Maple first opened its doors in 1862. The Gothic architecture is rather unique because of the extensive use of wood. Many of the church's features are much finer than they might otherwise be had they been rendered in more cumbersome stone.

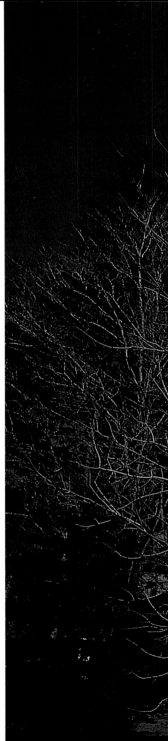

## Saint Paul's Anglican Church
### *Stormont, Dundas and Glengarry County*

All that remains now of the old Saint Paul's Anglican Church near Cardinal is this boarded-up tower that sits forlornly facing Highway 2. Completed in 1833, the church was built on the banks of the Saint Lawrence River on donated land. Attendance was limited, and a decision was made to relocate the church in Cardinal to better serve the Anglican population. In 1872 a new Saint Paul's was constructed and the old one dismantled, leaving the tower and graveyard as a remembrance.

## Saint John the Baptist Anglican Church
*Haliburton County*

Saint John the Baptist Anglican Church, constructed in 1887, sits attractively at the foot of a small treed bluff at Irondale. Irondale was once a thriving mining town and its decline has seen the loss of all important buildings except this church. Today Saint John the Baptist Church maintains services only seasonally.

## Saint Margaret's Chapel (Non-Denominational)
*Bruce County*

Saint Margaret's Chapel, near Dyers Bay, was completed in the early 1930s, making it one of our newer samples. Due to the economic hardships of the thirties, construction relied heavily on the donated time and efforts of many people. The windows were donated by a large glass company from London and the oak pews were provided by a wealthy widow. The solid-brass bell was salvaged from an old Grand Trunk Railroad train engine. Today Saint Margaret's occupies a secluded clearing on the Forty Hills Road. Its doors are always open, welcoming passers-by for rest and meditation in its quiet, rural atmosphere.

## Saint Mark's Anglican Church
*Northumberland County*

Saint Mark's Anglican Church in Port Hope has undergone many changes since it was first constructed in 1822. The original building was a modest rectangular structure. When first consecrated in 1828, it was dedicated to Saint John the Baptist. As the decades passed and the local population increased, galleries and transepts were added to accommodate the growing parish. In 1869 a new Saint John's was built and this church was closed. Re-opened in 1873, it was rededicated to Saint Mark and serves its own parish to this day.

## Wesleyan Methodist Church
### *Durham Region*

One of the few remaining buildings from the pioneer community of Glen Major, south of Uxbridge, is the Wesleyan Methodist Church. This board-and-batten structure was completed in 1873. Glen Major evolved around some grist and lumber mills. As the surrounding forest died out, so did the town. As is so often the case, the church survived and still holds seasonal services.

## Saint Philip's Church
*Thunder Bay District*

Although Saint Philip's Church is boarded up and padlocked, it continues to serve the Roman Catholics of Hymers. This frame church was constructed in the early 1930s and still celebrates Mass during the summer months.

## Barrie Island United Church
### *Manitoulin District*

Many buildings on Manitoulin Island stand in mute testimony of more populous and prosperous days. One is this deserted United church on Barrie Island, a township of District Manitoulin. A sign on the door warns visitors to use caution, as the doors are no longer on hinges. Inside, the pews and old stove are gone; the tattered old altar railing curtains are food for a growing community of moths. Remaining is a bookcase containing a few old books, some with publishing dates from the 1800s.

## The West Dumfries Chapel (Methodist)
*Brant County*

This unique cobblestone church near Paris was completed in 1845. Built by its own congregation, the church was erected using stones which were collected from the surrounding fields. This novel form of construction had been introduced to the vicinity a few years earlier by an American builder, Levi Boughton. The West Dumfries Chapel served the Methodist faithful until regular services ceased in 1921. Today the structure is beautifully maintained as a tribute to the history of the area.

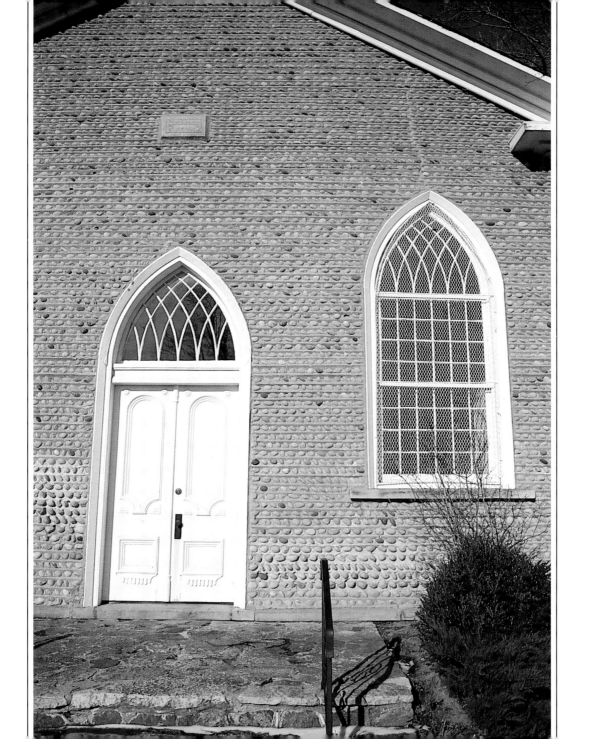

## Reesor Mennonite Church
*York Region*

The Reesor Mennonite Church has dominated the intersection of present-day Steeles Avenue and Pickering Town Line since 1820. The simple frame building, still in use, provides silent testimony to the Mennonites rustic and modest ways.

## Christ Church
## (Anglican)
### Essex County

The Anglican Christ Church in Amherstburg was built in 1818 and served as the garrison church for the officers and men of Fort Malden. The fort had been re-established to guard against the threat of further American aggression following the War of 1812. As tensions eased with time, Canada's need for a military presence on the Detroit River declined. Christ Church has since retired to more sedate civilian life and now attracts Amberstburg's Anglican flocks.

## Saint James' Roman Catholic Church
### *Simcoe County*

Saint James' Roman Catholic Church at Colgan is the third building to occupy this site. The parish was established with a simple log edifice in the early 1830s. As the local Catholic population grew, the need for a larger church became apparent. Today's Saint James' has towered over the crossroads of Colgan since 1888.

## Saint Andrew's Presbyterian
*York Region*

Just north of King City sits this small fieldstone church. Saint Andrew's Presbyterian is one of the last remaining vestiges of Eversley, a settlement which has now almost disappeared. The church was constructed in 1848 and remained active until 1958. As the town's population declined, so did the church's regular attendance. Today it is the picturesque setting for an occasional wedding.

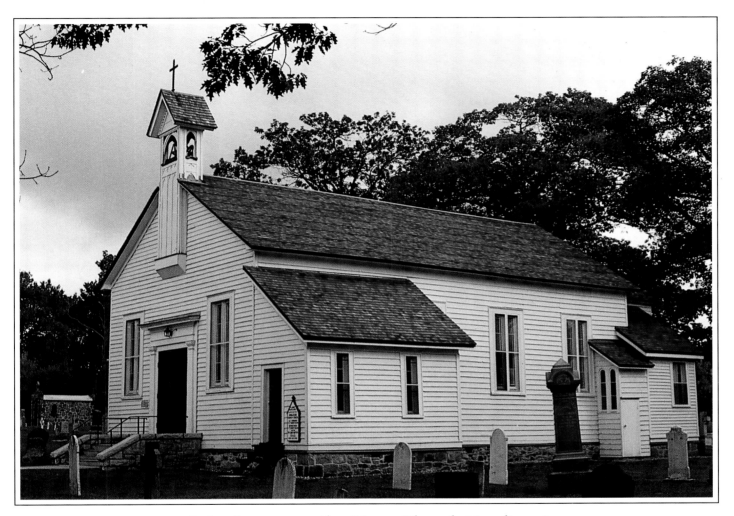

## Saint James-on-the-Lines Church (Anglican)
*Simcoe County*

Saint James-on-the-Lines Church is the garrison church that was built on the former Penetanguishene Military Reserve in 1838. It served both the military and civilian populations for 30 years as the only Protestant house of worship in the vicinity. Funding for the building is attributed to the efforts of Captain John Moberly, the establishment's naval commander.

## Saint Jude's Anglican Church
*Metropolitan Toronto*

Saint Jude's is the oldest church in Scarborough. Built in 1848 by the local Anglican congregation, the church was modelled after its first minister's former church in England. This building was replaced by a larger brick structure, where the regular Sunday services are now held. However the old frame Saint Jude's is still used for special occasions such as weddings and Easter services.

## Saint Andrew's Church
### Northumberland County

One of the oldest surviving Presbyterian churches in Ontario is Saint Andrew's Church in Colborne. This church was built in a classic Georgian design from local stone and completed in 1833. Eighty years later the church was graced with a taller bell tower and a Sunday School.

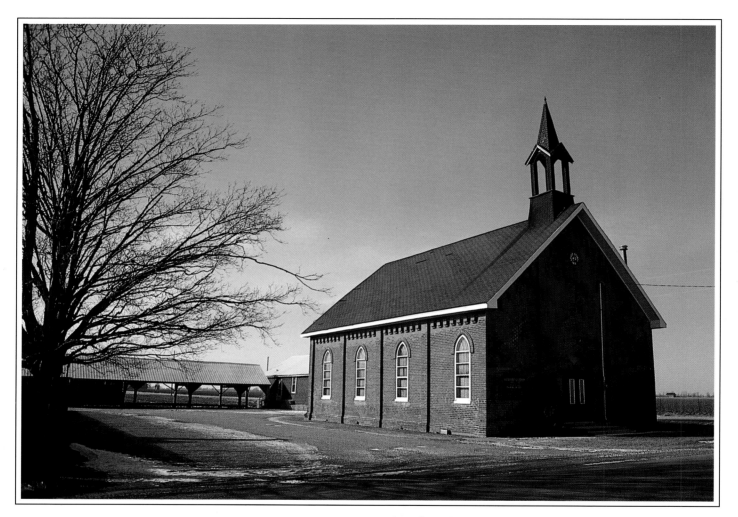

## Grace United
*Kent County*

In 1804 Lord Selkirk brought from Scotland over a hundred immigrants to settle an area near Wallaceburg. The people of Baldoon, as the settlement was named, suffered many setbacks before becoming established. Many of them died in the first year. This church, Grace United, built in 1881, dominates the crossroads at present-day Baldoon. We especially admired the interesting bell tower.

## Quaker Meeting House
*York Region*

The Quakers' preference for simplicity is demonstrated in this modest frame meeting house at Newmarket. The tombstones in the adjoining graveyard are small and unpretentious. Construction on this building began in 1810 on land located by William Doan, and the meeting house has held services ever since, making it the oldest place of worship in York Region.

## Saint Thomas' Anglican Church
### *Simcoe County*

Saint Thomas' Anglican, a Romanesque-style church in Shanty Bay, bears the distinction of being one of the few remaining churches constructed using the "rammed earth" method. In this process wet clay is mixed with straw and pressed into forms. When the clay dries, the blocks are sided with plaster or wood to protect them against the weather. Construction of this church started in 1838 and was completed in 1841.

## Madill Church
## (United)
### *Muskoka District*

The Methodist Church located near Huntsville is one of the last squared-timber churches remaining in Ontario. It was constructed by 1873 on land donated by John Madill, an early settler. Wesleyan Methodist missionaries held the first services in this church and the United Church maintains annual services.

## The Blue Church
*Leeds and Grenville County*

The land on which this church stands is a graveyard dating from at least 1790. Local Anglicans built a frame chapel here in 1809. In 1826 a new church in nearby Maitland took over its duties. The original structure burned and was dismantled in 1840. The small church we see today, known simply as "The Blue Church," was constructed in 1845 and beckons travellers to its peace and solitude from the side of the road near Prescott.

## Saint Isidore Roman Catholic Church
### *Thunder Bay District*

Saint Isidore Roman Catholic Church in Dorian was built in 1920. This little frame church and its adjoining graveyard are pictures of tranquility that reflect the quiet atmosphere of this small community. Saint Isidore still serves the Catholics of the area.

## Saint Mary's Church
*Middlesex County*

In the early 1830s a number of British army and navy veterans settled in the western Middlesex County area. Several years later one of these men donated land for a local church and cemetery. By 1843 this frame church, Saint Mary's, had been built to serve the needs of the local Anglicans. We were unable to determine the current status of the building, but the historical plaque outside attests that Saint Mary's is the oldest remaining church in Middlesex County.

## Salem Presbyterian Church
*Bruce County*

The Salem Presbyterian Church northwest of Chesley must have served its congregation for a relatively short period of time. Constructed in 1922, this solid, square brick structure with supporting buttresses was apparently meant to endure the elements for a long time. Today, however, it sits abandoned, in growing disrepair. The broken windows openly welcome the wind and precipitation, the church's only regular visitors. Ironically, the door is securely padlocked, yet the basement windows are broken, allowing easy access to anyone thus inclined.

## Saint Mary's Roman Catholic Church
### *York Region*

Just outside of the expanding community of Nobleton, perched atop a small hill, is Saint Mary's Roman Catholic Church. It was originally constructed as a small frame building and given the brick facade just prior to the turn of the century. It has ministered to the devoted since it opened in 1855.

## Saint Peters Anglican Church
*Elgin County*

Saint Peters Anglican Church near Wallacetown was accustomed to visits from some of Upper Canada's more prominent personalities. Built in 1827, this early Gothic Revival structure was consecrated by Bishop John Strachan in 1849. When the bell tower was added in 1845, the Earl of Galloway donated a bell to summon the faithful.

Lieutenant-Governor John Simcoe's daughter, Charlotte, donated a silver communion service. Colonel Thomas Talbot, the founder of the Talbot Settlement, and the man for whom the Talbot Trail was named, is interred in the church's burial ground.

## Sharon Temple
*York Region*

One of the most structurally interesting places of worship in Ontario is the Davidites' Sharon Temple at Sharon. David Willson left the Society of Friends in his native New York because of his controversial view on music and song. He established his sect, known as the Davidites, or the Children of Peace, at Sharon, where the temple was erected in 1832. The building's acoustics are exceptional and testify to the importance Willson placed on music as a form of prayer. The design of the building is such that there is no main entrance. All doors are of the same shape and size to signify that all persons entering are equal in the eyes of God. Although the Davidites dwindled to obscurity shortly after Willson's death in 1866, the Sharon Temple is still used for concerts and other special events.

## Wesleyville United Church
*Northumberland County*

We happened upon this building shortly after a rainstorm and were inspired by the freshly washed forested setting. This church is just west of Port Hope and the plaque on the front reads "Wesleyville United Church. 1860."

## Fisherville Presbyterian Church
*Metropolitan Toronto*

The busy intersection of Steeles Avenue and Dufferin Street, on the boundary between Metropolitan Toronto and York Region, was once the site of Fisherville. This simple Presbyterian church was erected there in 1856. Fisherville was eventually devoured by the urban sprawl of Toronto and the town is now remembered by a commemorative plaque in a cemetery near the intersection. In the early 1960s the church was moved, to join other historical buildings at Black Creek Pioneer Village, a few miles to the west.

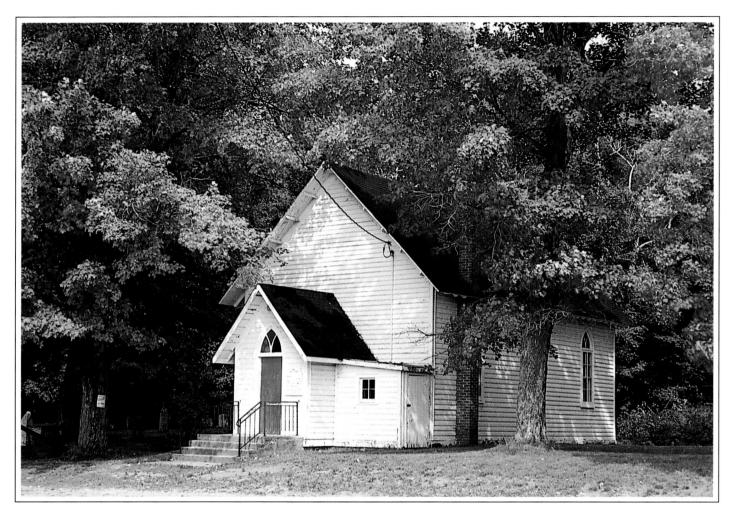

## Ebenezer United Church
*Parry Sound District*

In 1890 a congregation of local Methodists pooled their finances and combined their resources to produce this white frame church in the town of Nobel. Ebenezer United Church was constructed to provide a more formal place of worship for the faithful, who until then had been meeting at the Barker residence. Regular services have been maintained, and at the time of this writing, a celebration of its centennial was being prepared, an indication of the members' devotion to their church.

## Saint John's Lutheran Church
### Bruce County

Although the windows of this church are boarded up, the building appears to be in good shape. A sign identifies it as Saint John's Lutheran Church, established in 1876. It is located near Mildmay.

## Saint Pius V Roman Catholic Church
*Thunder Bay District*

Saint Pius V Roman Catholic Church was constructed in 1915 near the Stanley crossroads and served the area until the early 1980s. Today a mere shell, the church has suffered the ravages of weather and vandalism, and its tiny cemetery is overgrown with weeds.

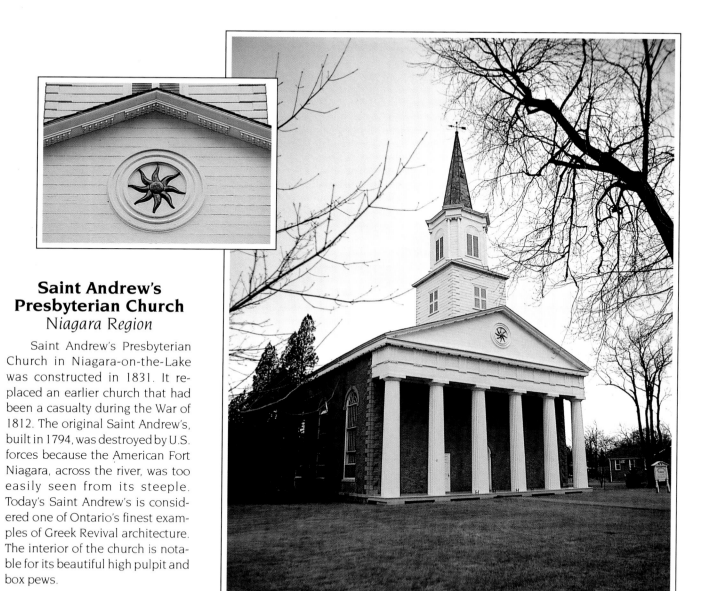

## Saint Andrew's Presbyterian Church
### Niagara Region

Saint Andrew's Presbyterian Church in Niagara-on-the-Lake was constructed in 1831. It replaced an earlier church that had been a casualty during the War of 1812. The original Saint Andrew's, built in 1794, was destroyed by U.S. forces because the American Fort Niagara, across the river, was too easily seen from its steeple. Today's Saint Andrew's is considered one of Ontario's finest examples of Greek Revival architecture. The interior of the church is notable for its beautiful high pulpit and box pews.

## Saint Luke's Anglican Church
### *Halton Region*

Though it appears to be modern, Saint Luke's Anglican Church in Burlington was built in 1834. As originally constructed, it was a plain frame building, but it has been subjected to many renovations over the years. The church is on one of the parcels of land which were granted to Chief Joseph Brant for his loyalty to the British Crown during the American Revolution.

## Her Majesty's Chapel of the Mohawks (Anglican)
*Brant County*

This book would be incomplete without inclusion of Her Majesty's Chapel of the Mohawks. Originally called Saint Paul's, this Anglican church was built in 1785 near present-day Brantford. It bears the distinction of being the first Protestant church constructed in Ontario, and is Ontario's oldest surviving church.

## Saint Andrew's-by-the-Lake Anglican Church
*Metropolitan Toronto*

The Toronto Islands have been providing a source of recreation for Toronto's citizenry for well over 100 years. But the islands are also home to a permanent, albeit declining, community. This early-English-Gothic-style frame church was opened in 1884 to serve the growing number of residents and cottagers. Aptly named, Saint Andrew's-by-the-Lake Anglican Church remains important to the islands' religious community.

## Relessey United Church
*Dufferin County*

The Relessey United Church, north of Orangeville, was constructed in 1870 to replace an earlier log structure that had dated from 1854. Originally built as a Wesleyan Methodist church, it was converted to the United faith in 1925. Of particular interest are the four spires atop its belfry, an architectural feature normally found on Anglican churches.

## Hay Bay Church
*Lennox and Addington County*

The first Methodist church in Upper Canada was built north of Adolphustown on Hay Bay in 1792 by United Empire Loyalists. It became the property of the United Church of Canada in 1925, and is that denomination's oldest church. Because it was one of the first permanent structures in the area, the church was also used for many secular functions. In 1795 trials were held there, and during the War of 1812 the church sheltered soldiers. In the late 1800s Hay Bay church was used for a time as a storehouse by a local farmer. In 1910 the building was purchased for the Methodist Church and eventually restored. Religious services are now being held there on a regular basis.

## Nicholson Catholic Church
### *Sudbury District*

Little is known of the origins of the Catholic church at Nicholson. Once a busy lumbering company town, Nicholson is now abandoned and yielding to a young forest. The Diocese of Sault Ste. Marie is in possession of a document signed by Bishop Dignan and decreeing that the name of this church would be Saint Nicholas of Tolentino. The letter is dated 3 April 1936. This was probably only a name change; there were several churches that received new names at that time, because of duplication. Today Nicholson's fate is being slowly sealed by vandalism and nature's forces. Little remains of the town's buildings save a few skeletal remains and piles of rotting lumber.

# Bibliography

Brown, Lindsey, *The Bruce; a Guide*. The Mariner Chart Shop, Tobermory, 1979.

Brown, Ron, *Backroads of Ontario*. Hurtig Publishers Ltd., Edmonton, 1984.

Brown, Ron, *Ghost Towns of Ontario. Volume 1*. Cannonbooks, Toronto, 1978.

*Loyal She Remains*. The United Empire Loyalists' Association of Canada, Toronto, 1984.

McCormick-Hooper, Marion, *Pelee Island Then and Now*. Herald Press Limited, Windsor, 1967.

*Ball's Falls Historical Park*. Niagara Peninsula Conservation Authority.

Ondaatje, Kim, *Small Churches of Canada*. Lester & Orpen Dennys, Toronto, 1982.

Reynolds, Arthur G., *The Story of the Hay Bay Church*. Hay Bay Church Board of Trustees, 1978.

Scanlon, J.P., *Olden Days at Moose Factory*.

The authors also gratefully acknowledge material provided by historical plaques erected by:
- Historical Sites and Monuments Board of Canada
- Ontario Archaeological and Historic Sites Board
- Ontario Heritage Foundation
- Roman Catholic Archdiocese of Toronto
- Scarborough Historical Society
- Toronto Historical Board

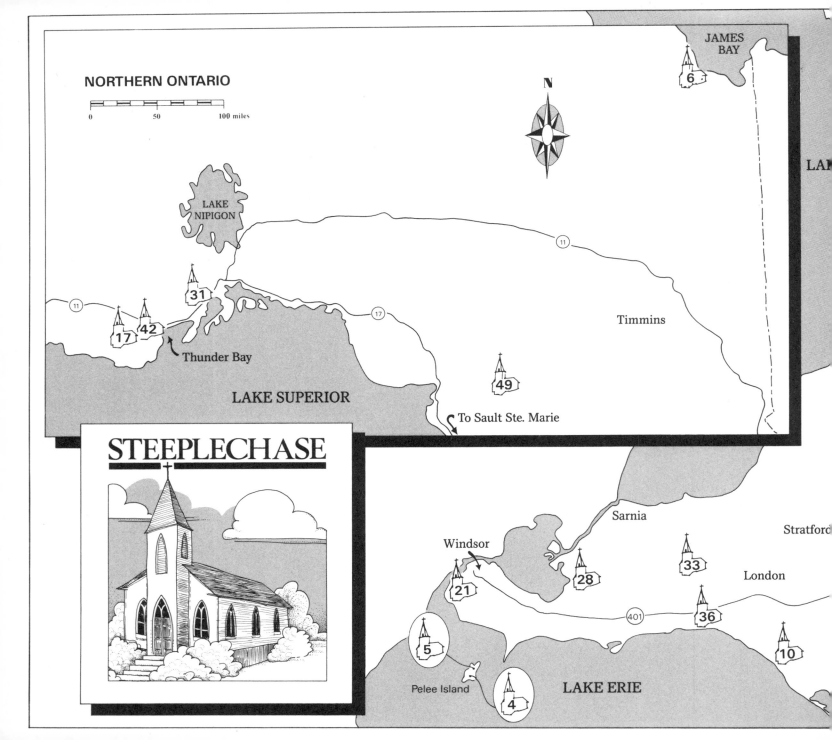

## NORTHERN ONTARIO

0    50    100 miles

JAMES BAY

**6**

LAKE

N

LAKE NIPIGON

11

**31**

11

17

**17** **42**

↑ Thunder Bay

Timmins

**49**

**LAKE SUPERIOR**

To Sault Ste. Marie

## STEEPLECHASE

Sarnia

Stratford

Windsor →

**21**

**28**

**33**

London

401

**36**

**5**

**10**

Pelee Island

**4**

**LAKE ERIE**